THE STORY OF THE
MILWAUKEE BUCKS

THE NBA:
A HISTORY
OF HOOPS

THE STORY OF THE
MILWAUKEE
BUCKS

SHANE FREDERICK

CREATIVE EDUCATION

Published by Creative Education
P.O. Box 227, Mankato, Minnesota 56002
Creative Education is an imprint of The Creative Company
www.thecreativecompany.us

Design and production by Blue Design
Art direction by Rita Marshall
Printed in the United States of America

Photographs by Corbis (Matt Brown/NewSport, MIKE
CASSESE/Reuters, Steve Lipofsky, JOE SKIPPER/Reuters,
FRED THORNHILL/Reuters), december.com (John
December), Getty Images (Brian Babineau/NBAE, Vernon
Biever/NBAE, Jonathan Daniel/Allsport, Gary Dineen/
NBAE, Focus on Sport, Walter Iooss Jr./NBAE, Heinz
Kluetmeier/Sports Illustrated, Ronald C. Modra/Sports
Imagery, Dick Raphael/NBAE, David Sherman/NBAE, Ron
Turenne/NBAE), Newscom (Harry E. Walker/MCT)

Library of Congress Cataloging-in-Publication Data
Frederick, Shane.
The story of the Milwaukee Bucks / Shane Frederick.
p. cm. — (The NBA: a history of hoops)
Includes index.
Summary: An informative narration of the Milwaukee
Bucks professional basketball team's history from its 1968
founding to today, spotlighting memorable players and
reliving dramatic events.
ISBN 978-1-60818-437-8
1. Milwaukee Bucks (Basketball team)—History—Juvenile
literature. I. Title.

GV885.52.M54F74 2014
796.323'640977595—dc23   2013039306

CCSS: RI.5.1, 2, 3, 8; RH.6-8.4, 5, 7

First Edition
9 8 7 6 5 4 3 2 1

Cover: Guard Brandon Knight
Page 2: Forward John Henson
Pages 4-5: Center Andrew Bogut
Page 6: Center Kareem Abdul-Jabbar

TABLE OF CONTENTS

COURTSIDE STORIES

INTRODUCING...

CELEBRATE GOOD TIMES

THE SCULPTURAL QUADRACCI PAVILION IS A FAMILIAR SIGHT IN TODAY'S MILWAUKEE.

Milwaukee, Wisconsin, is known as "The City of Festivals." Throughout the summer months, its citizens and many out-of-town visitors gather together outdoors to celebrate the city's rich cultural heritage and history through music, food, and art. Nearly every weekend there's something to celebrate in Milwaukee. When the festival season ends and the chill of winter begins to creep in, Wisconsinites still enjoy the outdoors. However, they also head inside, to places such as the Bradley Center, where they loyally cheer on the city's National Basketball Association (NBA) franchise, the Milwaukee Bucks.

The Bucks originated in Milwaukee as an expansion team in 1968. Led by guards Jon McGlocklin and Guy Rodgers, the club made its debut at the Milwaukee Arena on October 16, 1968. Although the Bucks lost a close contest

SWINGMAN OSCAR ROBERTSON LIVED UP TO HIS NUMBER (1) WITH ALL-AROUND SKILLS.

to the Chicago Bulls that night, they played in front of an excited crowd of 8,467 people. Those fans continued to support the Bucks despite Milwaukee's last-place finish in the Eastern Division.

The Bucks were awarded the top pick in the 1969 NBA Draft by virtue of a coin toss, and Milwaukee used that chance to select the best college player in the country, 7-foot-2 center Lew Alcindor. Alcindor's hanging jump shot, which became known as the "Sky Hook" in Milwaukee, had helped the University of California, Los Angeles (UCLA) win three college national championships. The Bucks

hoped the towering center could bring them the same kind of success.

With their new star leading the way, the Bucks turned into a winner. They ended their second season with a 56–26 record and a second-place finish in the division. Alcindor and fellow rookie Bob Dandridge, who played both forward and guard, led the Bucks to the division finals, where they were knocked out by the New York Knicks. But with Alcindor, the Bucks' future remained bright. "The big man is making us believe," McGlocklin said. "We're nobody's doormat anymore."

BIRDS OR BUCKS?

When the owners of the NBA's new Milwaukee franchise asked the people of Wisconsin to vote on a team name in 1968, they weren't surprised that their future fans had dozens of ideas, from skunks and beavers to stallions and stags. But they were shocked when the almost 15,000 votes were tallied and the number-one choice turned out to be the Robins. Instead of naming their team after a sweet and sunny songbird, owners Marvin Fishman and Wesley Pavalon decided to go with the second-place option: Bucks, after the mighty male white-tailed deer that are common in the woods of Wisconsin. R. D. Trebilcox, a fan from Whitefish Bay, Wisconsin, was 1 of almost 50 people who had suggested the name; he said it was fitting because "bucks are spirited, good jumpers, fast, and agile." Trebilcox won a new car—an AMC Javelin—for his suggestion. The name led to the creation of the original logo: a cartoonish buck wearing a green sweater with the letter *B* on it, which served as the team's official representation until 1993.

LEW ALCINDOR

(KAREEM ABDUL-JABBAR)
POSITION CENTER
HEIGHT 7-FOOT-2
BUCKS SEASONS
1969–75

Lew Alcindor—who became better known as Kareem Abdul-Jabbar—weighed 13 pounds when he was born on April 16, 1947. By the age of 14, he stood 7 feet tall and was already a star. When he was a freshman in high school, one of his team's games even had to be moved to New York City's Madison Square Garden to accommodate his fans! That was just a taste of what was to come for Alcindor, who grew both taller and more talented as time went by. The entire Milwaukee Bucks team was built around the mere possibility that it would be able to draft Alcindor after its inaugural season. It was the team's good fortune to win the first pick in the 1969 Draft—but luck had nothing to do with the Bucks' meteoric rise to an NBA championship just a year later. That was all Alcindor and his legendary "Sky Hook" shot. Although Alcindor went on to win five more NBA championships with the Los Angeles Lakers, his first was always his favorite. "Beating the Bullets in 1971 was tops," he said. "You can't do any better than that."

Before the start of the 1970–71 season, the Bucks brought in veteran forward/guard Oscar Robertson, who was nearing the end of his Hall of Fame career. "The Big O" proved he still had gas in the tank, setting a team record for assists (with 668) during the season. He and Alcindor led Milwaukee to a remarkable 66–16 record and a first-place finish in the newly formed Western Conference's Midwest Division.

The Bucks powered their way through the playoffs and into the 1971 NBA Finals by defeating both the San Francisco Warriors and the Los Angeles Lakers. That led to a Finals matchup against the Baltimore Bullets. Milwaukee swept the Bullets in four games to complete the team's amazing three-year rise to the top—the fastest climb to a league title in the history of professional sports. "That was really great," said Alcindor, who was named the NBA's Most Valuable Player (MVP) that year. "We won the world championship in the Bucks' third year of existence. That's something that I'll be proud of all of my life."

Before the 1971–72 season, Alcindor legally changed his name to Kareem Abdul-Jabbar to honor his Islamic faith. But nothing changed for the Bucks, who stormed to another first-

place finish with a stellar mark of 63–19, and Abdul-Jabbar, who had scored a team-record 55 points in a single game, picked up his second MVP award. In the playoffs, however, the Lakers avenged their previous postseason loss by beating the Bucks in the conference finals and going on to win the NBA Finals as well.

Behind the outstanding play of Robertson, Abdul-Jabbar, and guard Lucius Allen, the Bucks returned to the playoffs in both 1973 and 1974. Although they were eliminated by the Golden State Warriors in the first round in 1973, they fought their way back to the Finals in 1974, this time meeting the Boston Celtics. The two powerhouses split the first six games, but in Game 7, the Celtics pulled away for a 102–87 victory.

Robertson retired before the start of the 1974–75 season. With his supporting cast diminished, Abdul-Jabbar requested a trade before the 1975–76 season. After the Bucks dealt their star center to the Lakers, the team's glory days officially ended.

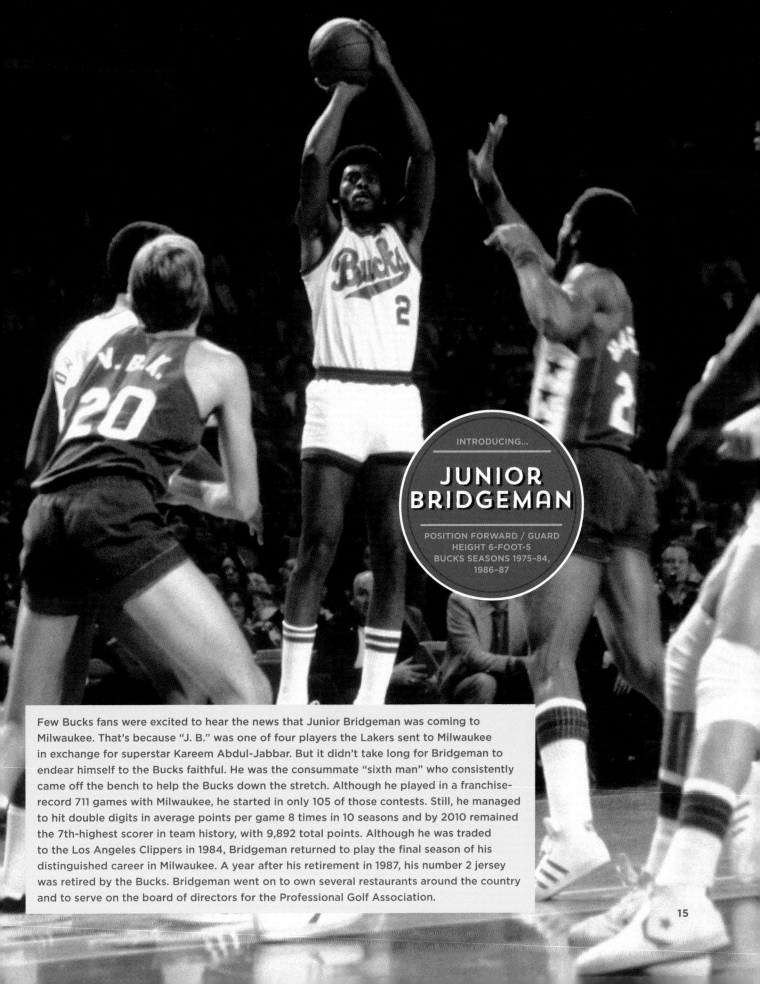

JUNIOR BRIDGEMAN

POSITION FORWARD / GUARD
HEIGHT 6-FOOT-5
BUCKS SEASONS 1975–84,
1986–87

Few Bucks fans were excited to hear the news that Junior Bridgeman was coming to Milwaukee. That's because "J. B." was one of four players the Lakers sent to Milwaukee in exchange for superstar Kareem Abdul-Jabbar. But it didn't take long for Bridgeman to endear himself to the Bucks faithful. He was the consummate "sixth man" who consistently came off the bench to help the Bucks down the stretch. Although he played in a franchise-record 711 games with Milwaukee, he started in only 105 of those contests. Still, he managed to hit double digits in average points per game 8 times in 10 seasons and by 2010 remained the 7th-highest scorer in team history, with 9,892 total points. Although he was traded to the Los Angeles Clippers in 1984, Bridgeman returned to play the final season of his distinguished career in Milwaukee. A year after his retirement in 1987, his number 2 jersey was retired by the Bucks. Bridgeman went on to own several restaurants around the country and to serve on the board of directors for the Professional Golf Association.

RUNS LIKE A DEER

CENTER BOB LANIER USED A SWEEPING LEFT-HANDED HOOK SHOT TO DOMINATE INSIDE.

DON NELSON

Although they were undeniably weakened by the loss of Abdul-Jabbar, the Bucks refused to give up. The scoring of Dandridge and new guard Brian Winters kept Milwaukee competitive in 1975–76. The team captured the division again, despite ending the season with only 38 wins, but lost to the Detroit Pistons in the first round of the playoffs.

The last member of the original Bucks squad, Jon McGlocklin, then retired, and, after Milwaukee went 3–15 in the first month of the season, head coach Larry Costello resigned. Assistant coach Don Nelson then took over and ushered in a new era in Bucks basketball. Although it was too late to salvage the 1976–77 campaign, Nelson and the Bucks entered the following season with a renewed sense of urgency.

So intense was the Bucks' desire to win that, in a

DON NELSON

With 540 victories, Don Nelson was the winningest head coach in Milwaukee Bucks history as of 2014. But he wasn't sure he was ready for the job when he was asked to take the position at the age of 36. "I expected to be an assistant at least two years, maybe longer, before trying for a head coaching job," he said at the time. "I don't have the most experience in the world." What the former NBA forward did have, though, was an innovative approach to basketball, which ultimately changed the way the game is played. He introduced the concept of the "point forward" to the game, in which a small forward directed the offense instead of a guard. His hallmark fast-paced offense, known as "Nellie Ball," is now employed by many other teams at every level of play. But it wasn't just on the court that Nelson shook things up; he was known to employ unusual motivational tactics in the locker room as well. To inspire his players before a game in 1984, he sang "Dig a Little Deeper in the Well," a song by the country and gospel quartet known as the Oak Ridge Boys.

game on November 25, 1977, they mounted the greatest single-game comeback in NBA history. Down 111–82 to the Atlanta Hawks with 8 minutes and 43 seconds remaining, the Bucks outscored Atlanta 35–4 down the stretch—led by "super sub" forward Junior Bridgeman, who scored 24 points in 26 minutes, and forward Marques Johnson, who hit 2 free throws in the final second to give the Bucks a 117–115 victory.

That was 1 of 44 wins Milwaukee notched on its way back to the playoffs. Although the Bucks missed the postseason altogether in 1978–79, they traded for future Hall of Fame center Bob Lanier during the next season. The 6-foot-11 and 250-pound Lanier then led the Bucks to five straight division titles. When the 1983–84 season ended, however, Lanier retired—without a championship ring. "Basketball is a game because it's fun, and it's a job because I get paid," he said. "I don't need a championship to have made my career a successful one."

Looking for a new team leader, the Bucks turned to 6-foot-3 guard Sidney Moncrief. Moncrief had been the Bucks' first-round draft pick in 1979 and had developed into an All-Star. Extraordinarily quick and agile, Moncrief was without peer as a defensive stopper. "That guy is amazing," said Celtics star forward Larry Bird. "It's obvious he takes pride in doing whatever it takes to win."

Moncrief led the Bucks as far as the Eastern Conference finals twice. But "Sir Sid" could not win by himself. With the help of forwards Terry Cummings and Paul Pressey, Moncrief and the speedy Bucks won the division two more years in a row and made it to the Eastern Conference finals again in 1986. Although the Bucks had

the 6-foot-11 Jack Sikma at center, their lack of size at all other positions crippled them in the playoffs. Frustrated by his inability to lead Milwaukee back to a championship, Coach Nelson stepped down in 1987.

Under new coach Del Harris, Milwaukee's win total in 1987–88 slipped below 50 for the first time since the beginning of the decade. Still, the Bucks drew more than 452,000 total fans to the Milwaukee Arena, which was replaced by the brand-new Bradley Center the following season. And they made it to—but not past—the first round of the playoffs.

The names on the roster changed substantially in the next few years, yet the Bucks remained a perennial playoff contender. But apart from a run to the second round of the postseason in 1989, Milwaukee was routinely eliminated in the first round. Moncrief left the team in 1990, signaling the end of another era in Milwaukee. "It's a shame we never won a championship with those teams," Moncrief reflected. "We always had championship heart."

PIONEER OF THE PROFESSION

On March 6, 1972, the Milwaukee Bucks named Wayne Embry the team's general manager. The former All-Star center, who had finished his 11-year NBA playing career with the Bucks, became the first African American general manager in NBA history. After seven seasons with the Bucks (and after orchestrating the infamous trade of star Kareem Abdul-Jabbar), Embry left in 1979 and went on to serve as general manager of the Cleveland Cavaliers and the Toronto Raptors. Along the way, he set an example for other black athletes looking for opportunities in the business of sports. "Wayne was the first walking, talking, breathing African American who showed he could run not just a basketball team but multimillion-dollar businesses," said former NBA player and coach Sam Mitchell. Embry was aware that he had been given a rare opportunity when the Milwaukee job was offered to him, and he worked as hard as he could to succeed. "I just refused to fail," he said. "It was imperative that I succeed. If I hadn't, I don't know how long it would have been for the people who came after me."

REBUILDING BUCKS

IN MARQUES JOHNSON'S 7 SEASONS WITH THE BUCKS, HE POSTED 10,980 POINTS.

The 1991–92 season marked the start of a much less prosperous era for the Milwaukee Bucks. Despite bringing in veteran center Moses Malone to boost its offensive numbers, the team struggled. The bright spot came when the team scored a total of 53 points in the fourth quarter of a November game against the Cleveland Cavaliers—a new club record. Unfortunately, that game was among the 51 that the Bucks lost that season. For the first time in more than a decade, Milwaukee landed in last place in its division—the Eastern Conference's Central Division—and for the first time in 12 years, the team missed the playoffs.

When the Bucks returned to the Bradley Center for the 1992–93 season, they found a new coach on the bench—former guard Mike Dunleavy—and seven new names on the roster, including guards Todd Day and Lee Mayberry and

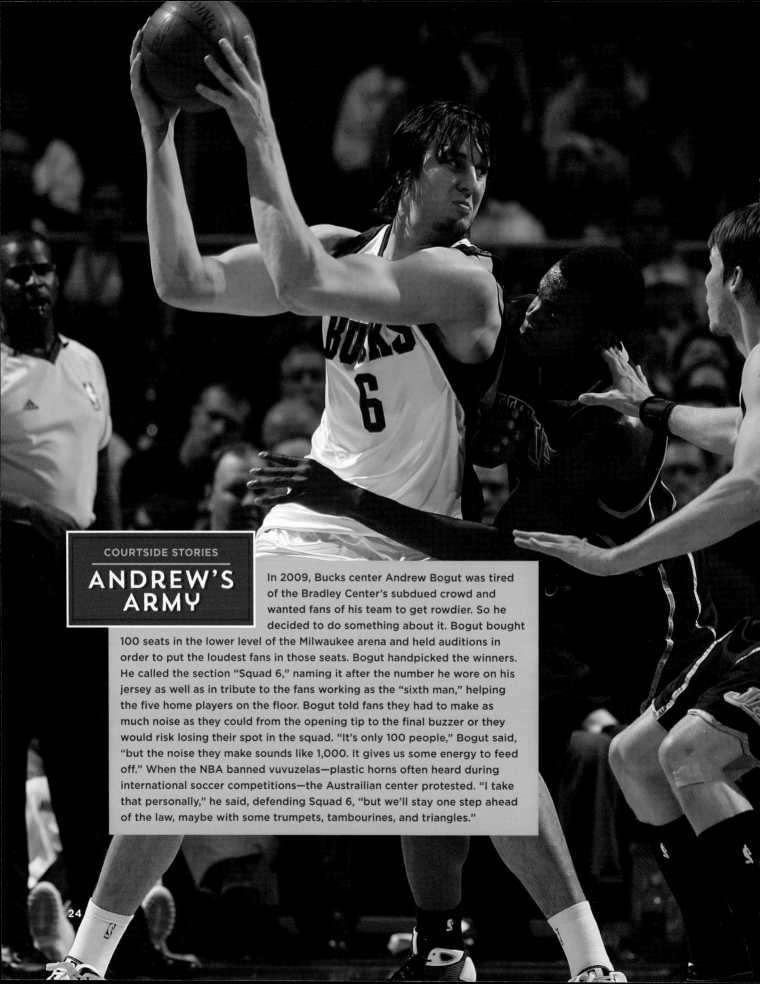

COURTSIDE STORIES

ANDREW'S ARMY

In 2009, Bucks center Andrew Bogut was tired of the Bradley Center's subdued crowd and wanted fans of his team to get rowdier. So he decided to do something about it. Bogut bought 100 seats in the lower level of the Milwaukee arena and held auditions in order to put the loudest fans in those seats. Bogut handpicked the winners. He called the section "Squad 6," naming it after the number he wore on his jersey as well as in tribute to the fans working as the "sixth man," helping the five home players on the floor. Bogut told fans they had to make as much noise as they could from the opening tip to the final buzzer or they would risk losing their spot in the squad. "It's only 100 people," Bogut said, "but the noise they make sounds like 1,000. It gives us some energy to feed off." When the NBA banned vuvuzelas—plastic horns often heard during international soccer competitions—the Austrailian center protested. "I take that personally," he said, defending Squad 6, "but we'll stay one step ahead of the law, maybe with some trumpets, tambourines, and triangles."

swingman Theodore "Blue" Edwards. Although Edwards rose to the challenge of carrying the team (he and forward/center Frank Brickowski led the Bucks in scoring, each with an average of 16.9 points per game), the other youngsters, such as Day and Mayberry, struggled. The Bucks finished in last place again, this time with a miserable 28–54 record.

The 1993–94 season started with a new look, as the Bucks' familiar green uniforms with the caricatured deer logo were replaced by purple jerseys emblazoned with a stylized buck. But other than the addition of energetic forward Vin Baker, the team's first-round draft pick in 1993, everything else in Milwaukee looked too much the same. The Bucks posted their worst record to date, winning only 20 games.

That dismal record turned into a golden opportunity when the Bucks won the right to make the first overall pick in the 1994 NBA

ATHLETIC BRUISER FRANK BRICKOWSKI NABBED REBOUNDS AND CAPITALIZED DOWN LOW.

FIT FOR A PRINCE

When you think of basketball royalty, you probably think of Michael Jordan or Magic Johnson. But what about Luc Mbah a Moute (*BAH-ah-MOO-tay*)? Well, the Bucks forward actually is royalty. He's a prince from the African village of Bia Messe, Cameroon, which is near the country's capital of Yaounde. Mbah a Moute's father is the elected village chief. "I didn't have people throwing rose petals at myself or things like that," he said, "but I definitely enjoyed being the prince of a chief." Mbah a Moute grew up playing soccer and didn't learn to play basketball until he was 12. He later moved to the United States, first to attend a high school in Florida and then college at the University of California, Los Angeles. After three years of playing basketball for the UCLA Bruins, he entered the 2008 NBA Draft, and Milwaukee selected him in the second round. When his NBA career ends, Mbah a Moute would like to return to Cameroon. "I'd like to move back there and be an ambassador for my country to teach everyone how beautiful it is."

> ## "YOU THINK YOU'RE DOING PRETTY WELL AGAINST THIS KID, AND THEN YOU LOOK UP AND HE'S GOT 20 POINTS."
>
> — TIMBERWOLVES GUARD DOUG WEST ON RAY ALLEN

Draft. In an effort to improve their scoring (they had averaged a franchise-low 96.9 points per game in 1993–94), the Bucks chose Glenn "Big Dog" Robinson, a 6-foot-7 forward from Purdue University who had been college basketball's National Player of the Year the previous season. The Bucks signed Robinson to a staggering 10-year, $68-million contract, but his teammates agreed that he was worth it. "We know what he can do for us, for this team, for this city," Baker said. "We will all be delighted to see him."

Robinson quickly became an impact player who could score from anywhere on the floor. In his rookie season, he led the team—and all NBA rookies—with 21.9 points per game. Although Robinson was named to the NBA All-Rookie team and Baker was an All-Star in 1994–95, the Bucks missed the playoffs for the fourth consecutive season. With a 25–57 record the following year, they finished in last place once again.

At season's end, Coach Dunleavy was fired, but before he left, he orchestrated a draft-day trade with the Minnesota Timberwolves that sent rookie guard Ray Allen to Milwaukee instead of Minnesota. Allen's smooth but deadly style, as well as his remarkable accuracy from the three-point line, caught many opponents unaware. "You think you're doing pretty well against this kid, and then you look up and he's got 20 points," said Timberwolves guard Doug West.

Under new coach Chris Ford, Allen and the Bucks jumped out to a promising start in 1996–97, going 15–11 before Christmas. But they returned from the holidays with a five-game losing streak and couldn't maintain the momentum that had been built during the first two months of the season. The Bucks posted a 33–49 record, well out of playoff contention.

SIDNEY MONCRIEF

POSITION GUARD
HEIGHT 6-FOOT-3
BUCKS SEASONS
1979–89

Sidney Moncrief had several nicknames, from "Sir Sid" to "Sid the Squid." But most Milwaukee Bucks fans remember him fondly as "Mr. Everything," the man who could shoot and slash, pass and post, and grab a rebound or two as well. For a decade, Moncrief was the biggest Buck in town, the undisputed leader of a team that was always a postseason contender. He scored almost 12,000 total points and nabbed nearly 3,500 rebounds during his career. His leadership earned him the respect of his teammates, and his relentless presence on the court earned him the admiration of his opponents. Chicago Bulls Hall-of-Famer Michael Jordan was among those who dreaded facing him. "When you play against Moncrief, you're in for a night of all-around basketball," the guard said. "He'll hound you everywhere you go, both ends of the court. You just expect it." Moncrief expected to win a championship with the Bucks, but he left in 1990 without a ring. He retired after playing one year for the Atlanta Hawks, and later became a coach. In 2011, Moncrief returned to Milwaukee to work as an assistant to Scott Skiles and Jim Boylan.

ON BIG DOG'S BACK

THE BUCKS LOOKED TO BIG DOG ROBINSON TO LEAD THE WAY INTO THE POSTSEASON.

I n 1997, Baker—who had grown unhappy with his compensation in comparison with Robinson's—was traded to the Seattle SuperSonics. The following year, Ford was fired, and George Karl, who had been coaching Baker in Seattle, was hired to take over as head coach. "This team has talent," Karl said, "but they need to play together and learn defensive discipline."

During the strike-shortened 1998–99 season, Karl integrated even more talent into the team's fabric. Point guard Sam Cassell, a plucky leader and solid shooter, and athletic forward Tim Thomas were both acquired through midseason trades. Although only 50 games were played, the improved Bucks posted their first winning record in 7 seasons and finally returned to the postseason.

The Indiana Pacers quickly swept the Bucks in the first round of the playoffs, but that taste of postseason play

POSTPONED DUE TO WEATHER

The Bucks have had to delay or postpone games four times because of wild wintry weather—but only once for conditions in Milwaukee itself. In 1982, a January game scheduled against the Atlanta Hawks had to be postponed when a storm dropped two inches of snow in Georgia, and several of the Hawks players could not get to the arena. Then a 1985 game against the Detroit Pistons was postponed when snow and ice crashed through the roof of Detroit's Silverdome, covering both the court and the stands. And in January 2007, bad weather stalled the New Orleans Hornets' flight from Oklahoma City, forcing the matchup to be played in April instead. The only time Wisconsin weather caused a problem was on January 8, 1989, when heavy fog in Milwaukee compelled the team's plane to land in Grand Rapids, Michigan, where the Bucks boarded a bus for an exhausting four-and-a-half hour drive home. Their game against the Utah Jazz started more than an hour late, but the Bucks managed to pull out a 107–89 win.

was intoxicating to the team. With Robinson, Allen, and Cassell combining for an incredible 5,008 points—more than 60 percent of the team's total scoring—the Bucks battled back to a 42–40 record in 1999–2000. Once again, they faced the Pacers and their star, guard Reggie Miller, in the playoffs.

The Bucks and Pacers split the first 4 games of the series, which included a Game 4 victory for Milwaukee at home that came 10 years to the day after the team's last postseason home win. But the deciding Game 5 was played in Indiana, where the Pacers clung to a 96–95 lead as Allen launched a desperation jumper at the

buzzer that bounced off the backboard. The Bucks returned to Milwaukee heartbroken but still hopeful. "We played them tough," a somber Robinson noted. "But a loss like this makes us realize we can do great things."

Despite Milwaukee's 3–9 start to the 2000–01 season, Robinson appeared determined to live up to his earlier statement. He and Allen both averaged 22 points per game, and Cassell dropped in another 18.2. By the end of the season, the team had posted a 52–30 record and claimed its first division crown since 1986.

This time, Milwaukee matched up against the Orlando Magic and star forward Tracy McGrady

RAY ALLEN

Ray Allen once said that he was "borderline obsessive compulsive." He always arrived at the arena early to practice—usually before anyone else was even in the building. That tendency helped explain his incredibly accurate shooting and his almost flawless form. Although Allen was an effective all-around scorer, he was particularly deadly from the three-point line. In his 7 seasons in Milwaukee, he sank 1,051 three-point field goals—an amazing .406 percentage of the 2,587 he attempted. In 2001, he won the Three-Point Shootout contest during the NBA All-Star Game weekend festivities. Allen was also a smooth and confident guard who inspired those around him. Although he never won a championship ring in Milwaukee, Allen eventually did make it to the NBA Finals with the Boston Celtics and was an important part of that team's championship in 2008. In the meantime, he also took up acting, landing one of the lead roles in the 1998 film *He Got Game*, about a high school basketball phenom. Film critic Roger Ebert praised Allen for his performance in the movie, calling him "a rarity: an athlete who can act."

35

in the first round of the playoffs. The Bucks easily took the first two games, then dropped the third in overtime, 121–116. In the next game, Allen scored 26 points and led the team to a 112–104 series-clinching victory. Allen and the Bucks then battled the Charlotte Hornets for seven games in the next round, winning the first two and the final two games. Robinson, who led the team with 29 points in the Game 7 victory, was overwhelmed by the series win. "I've looked at [Michael] Jordan, Magic [Johnson], and [Larry] Bird, knowing they played their whole careers for one team," he said. "They took their team to the next level, and that's what I've always wanted to do."

he next level for the Bucks was the Eastern Conference finals, where they were pitted against a Philadelphia 76ers team that was also eager to get back to the NBA Finals after an almost 20-year absence. It was a hard-fought series, but in the deciding Game 7, 76ers guard Allen Iverson scored 44 points as the Bucks lost, 108–91.

The deflated Bucks were hampered the following season by injuries to the team's 5

top scorers: Allen, Robinson, Cassell, Thomas, and guard Michael Redd combined to miss a total of 56 games. Even as a record number of fans crowded into the Bradley Center for home games, the crippled team fell to 41–41 and missed the playoffs by just one game. Their brief return to the postseason in 2003 was a last hurrah for the nucleus of players that had tried so hard to turn the team's fortunes around. By the time the 2003–04 season started, Allen, Robinson, Cassell, and Coach Karl were all gone.

DESPITE A SOLID SHOWING OVER FIVE FULL SEASONS, TIM THOMAS WAS TRADED TO THE KNICKS IN 2004.

IN THE HUNT

MICHAEL REDD'S STRONG, ON-TARGET SHOOTING CATAPULTED HIM INTO THE SPOTLIGHT.

Milwaukee started filling the gaping holes in its roster by selecting speedy point guard T. J. Ford in the 2003 NBA Draft. The team had also picked up veteran forward Keith Van Horn from the New Jersey Nets. But it was guard Michael Redd who emerged from his longtime role as a sub to start all 82 games and lead the team with 21.7 points per game.

Redd's development as a sharpshooting, everyday player was particularly important after Ford collided with Timberwolves forward Mark Madsen on February 24, 2004. Ford fell to the floor and lost feeling in his arms and legs; he had to be strapped to a gurney and wheeled out of the arena with what was later diagnosed as a bruised spinal cord. The young point guard was lost for the season and missed the team's trip to the playoffs, where the Pistons

HEAD COACH SCOTT
SKILES STRESSED DEFENSE
AND CONSISTENCY TO HIS
BUCKS PLAYERS.

knocked off the Bucks, four games to one.

ord didn't make it back for the 2004–05 season, either, after undergoing surgery to fuse two of his vertebrae. As the team soldiered through a subpar 30–52 season without him, he contemplated the odds of making a complete recovery. "We all know you can't play forever," Ford said during his long rehabilitation. "So I do understand that I never know when it's my last day of playing. Last year could have been my last day."

Fortunately for the Bucks, Ford was able to return in 2005–06, and he was joined by free-agent forward Bobby Simmons, a versatile young player who added depth to the roster. But even more exciting was the team's opportunity to make the first choice in the 2005 NBA Draft. With it, the Bucks chose Andrew Bogut, a seven-foot center from Australia who possessed great passing skills for a player of his size. "The people of Milwaukee, no matter what, they do everything very, very hard," Bogut said. "That's exactly like I am. When I do something, I go full steam. I respect a city that prides itself on hard work."

INTRODUCING...

BRANDON JENNINGS

**POSITION POINT GUARD
HEIGHT 6-FOOT-1
BUCKS SEASONS
2009–13**

Brandon Jennings was considered the best high school basketball player in the country, playing for Virginia's Oak Hill Academy in 2008. But that year, rules were changed, and prep players were no longer allowed to make the jump directly to the NBA, as stars such as Kevin Garnett and Kobe Bryant had done. Rather than go to college, Jennings moved to Italy, where he signed on to play professionally for one year with Lottomatica Virtus Roma. He didn't get a lot of playing time that season, but he did enough to impress the Bucks, who drafted him with the 10th overall pick in the summer of 2009. Just seven games into his NBA career, Jennings proved Milwaukee's scouts right. That night, he scored 55 points in a 129–125 win over the Golden State Warriors. That broke the Bucks' rookie record of 51 points set by Lew Alcindor and was just 2 points shy of Michael Redd's franchise-record 57-point game. Former Bucks coach Don Nelson, who was coaching Golden State that night, called it "probably the best rookie performance I've ever witnessed in 30-some years of coaching."

AS A ROOKIE, BRANDON
JENNINGS AVERAGED 15.5
POINTS, 5.7 ASSISTS, AND
3.4 BOARDS.

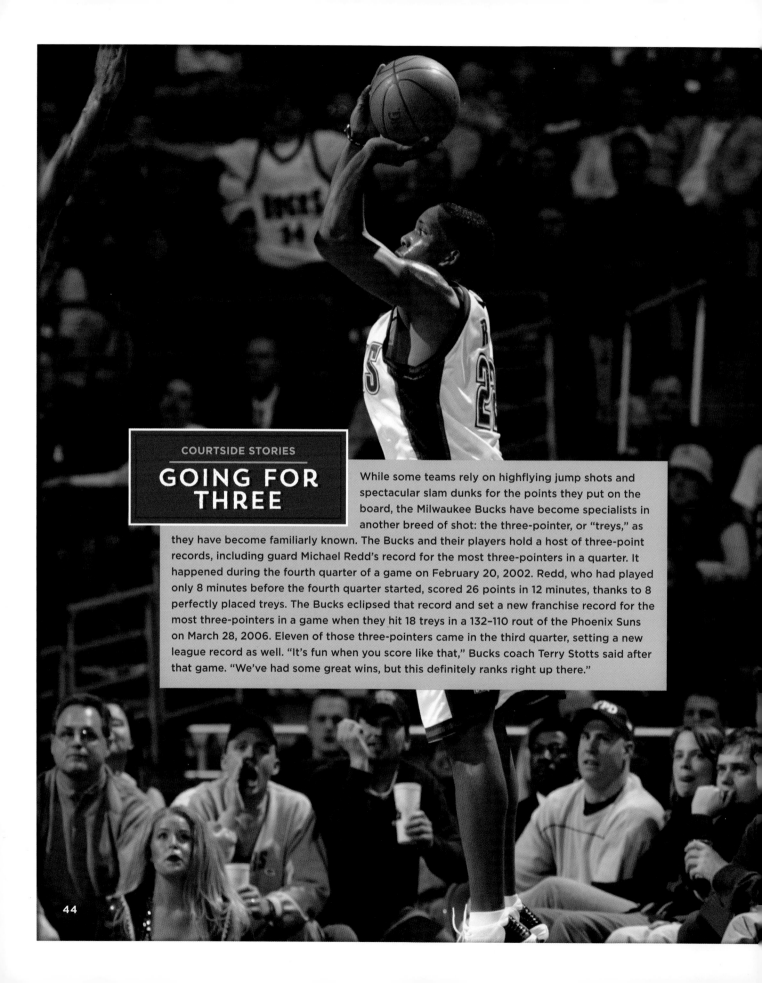

GOING FOR THREE

While some teams rely on highflying jump shots and spectacular slam dunks for the points they put on the board, the Milwaukee Bucks have become specialists in another breed of shot: the three-pointer, or "treys," as they have become familiarly known. The Bucks and their players hold a host of three-point records, including guard Michael Redd's record for the most three-pointers in a quarter. It happened during the fourth quarter of a game on February 20, 2002. Redd, who had played only 8 minutes before the fourth quarter started, scored 26 points in 12 minutes, thanks to 8 perfectly placed treys. The Bucks eclipsed that record and set a new franchise record for the most three-pointers in a game when they hit 18 treys in a 132–110 rout of the Phoenix Suns on March 28, 2006. Eleven of those three-pointers came in the third quarter, setting a new league record as well. "It's fun when you score like that," Bucks coach Terry Stotts said after that game. "We've had some great wins, but this definitely ranks right up there."

After making a quick exit from the playoffs that year, Bogut and the Bucks remained mired at the bottom of the their division following three seasons, missing the postseason every year despite the efforts of guards Charlie Bell and Mo Williams. A turnaround finally began in Milwaukee in 2009–10. That season, new coach Scott Skiles oversaw a reshaped roster featuring Redd, Bogut, sharpshooting guard John Salmons, and ultra-quick rookie point guard Brandon Jennings. That lineup reenergized Milwaukee by charging to a 46–36 record. Then, despite the absence of Bogut and Redd (both of whom suffered injuries during the season), the undermanned Bucks nearly toppled the Hawks in a seven-game playoff series. "We did the best we could," Jennings said after the series. "We showed a lot of people that the Milwaukee Bucks can actually hang in this league."

ilwaukee couldn't keep the momentum going, though. The Bucks missed the playoffs the next two years, so the talented Bogut was told goodbye in 2012. The Bucks traded him to the Warriors for 20-points-per-game shooting guard Monta Ellis. While the combination of Ellis and Jennings gave Milwaukee the potential of having a high-scoring backcourt, some wondered if the two players would be able to share the ball. "We said we'll sacrifice whatever just to win," Jennings said. "So if he's got it going that night, he's got it going. If I've got it going, whatever. We don't even have to score that many points. As long as we're winning and everybody's happy, that's fine with us."

Ellis and Jennings averaged nearly 37 points per game combined in 2012–13, while third-year forward Larry Sanders developed into a defensive force. After Jim Boylan replaced Skiles during a midseason coaching change, the Bucks returned to the playoffs. They were quickly dispatched in a four-game sweep by the mighty Miami Heat.

The Bucks were in for a serious off-season shake-up. Former Atlanta Hawks coach Larry Drew took the helm as the majority of the roster, including Jennings, was dealt away or signed with other clubs. In 2013–14, Milwaukee went on to post a miserable record, but there were bright spots of scoring from guards Brandon Knight and O. J. Mayo as well as forward Khris Middleton. Greek swingman Giannis Antetokounmpo was pegged as a young player to watch. Despite the disappointing year, a number of late-season victories renewed fans' hopes for the future.

Throughout the history of the Milwaukee Bucks, fans have experienced many ups and downs, from an early NBA title to more recent battles to get into the playoffs. But they are waiting patiently and believe that it is only a matter of time before their Bucks bound back to championship status. And that will give their festive city yet another reason to celebrate.

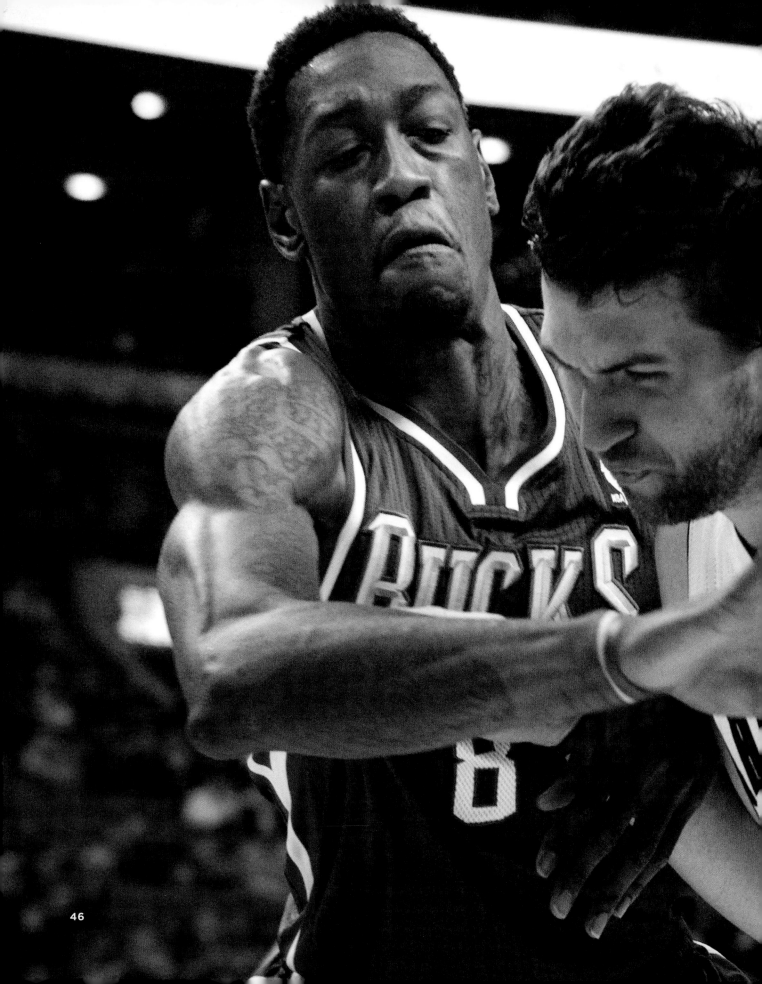

LARRY SANDERS BOOSTED THE BUCKS' DEFENSE WITH 201 BLOCKS IN 2012–13.

INDEX